SPIRITUALLY
CIRCUMCISE
Your
HEART & MIND

TIMOTHY L. WALKER

&

Inspired by the Holy Spirit & Prayer

authorHOUSE®

AuthorHouse™
1663 Liberty Drive
Bloomington, IN 47403
www.authorhouse.com
Phone: 1 (800) 839-8640

Published by AuthorHouse   06/27/2016

ISBN: 978-1-5246-0547-6 (sc)
ISBN: 978-1-5246-0545-2 (hc)
ISBN: 978-1-5246-0546-9 (e)

Library of Congress Control Number: 2016906702

Print information available on the last page.

Table of Contents

FOREWORD

For over the past Sixteen years I have been in the process of writing what God has put on my Heart and Mind, of course with time both has been through a lot of things because of changes in my life, but most importantly the process of being circumcised of the "Norms" of what is being taught in most Sunday Schools, Pulpits and by Traditions of Men I had to separate myself from that. I'm not saying I am holier-than-thou, but when "Truth" has resonated in your Heart and Mind you have to adhere to what the Holy Spirit leads and guides you; therefore the core of what was given to me is now in full labor being birth on paper. I cannot hold back, I have to let out so God can replenish me with a fresh revelation of His Word and Plan for Mankind. The Bible for me is the *(Basic Instructions Before Living Eternally)*, inspired by God's Holy Spirit and Jesus the Word fore-filled it!

God's Word never changes, but it will impregnate your mind and when it does, don't be afraid to give birth to it for Mary gave birth to "The Word." My desire is that this book will open eyes and understanding too many, even answer questions; but most importantly is that it will dive you into the Word, then the Word will pierce your Heart and Mind to be more acceptance to have Communion with the Father, Son and Holy Spirit.

Remember Jesus said in ***Mark 13:13*** *"And ye shall be hated of all men for my name's sake: but he that shall endure unto the end, the same shall be saved." (Note: the opposite of the statement is if you don't endure unto the end you will not be saved).* Therefore, take heed and guard the gateway to your Ears and Eyes, because it affects your Heart and Mind; if not, the Holy Spirit will have to perform Spiritual Circumcision to bring you back in line with God's Word. God is (Guarantee of Deliverance) for whoever believes In and On Jesus Christ and because of God's Love (Level of Victory Eternally), they will have Eternal Life with Him right here on Earth after He rejuvenates it.

If you ask the question where is "Our People" in the Bible, you must understand it was and still is instructions for God's chosen people (Hebrews/Israelites) and the story of those who came in contact with them. If you are not of Hebrew/Israelite decent, but have accepted Jesus Christ as your Lord and Savior you are adopted into all the Promises

& Covenant of God. If you cannot or do not understand the "Beginning" of anything you are reading or have read; then how can you fully understand the Plot of the story for which it was written for, then you will not have a clear understanding of the Ending.

I write this book for Christians and Spiritual Minded people who are in search for the deeper Truths of the Bible, God's Eternal Plan for Salvation *and* "Whoever Believes In and On Jesus Christ" that wants to keep their Amour properly shined so they can Stand and Faint not when "Satan's Fiery Darts" come their way and especially if they are alive when "The Anti-Christ" (Satan) shows up on earth with his angles. Therefore, they will be able to spiritually discern rather what they believe in is totally Truth or Traditions of Men. In addition, I want to clear up some Norms that are preached and taught in many churches that are very misleading, because most people believe that whatever the Pastor(s) say or have said are Truths.

Just remembering that Satan himself quotes scriptures, but always has a twist on it that sounds good and if you don't study to show thyself approved before God you will fall for a lie. Satan tried to use the Word of God against the "Word" born in the flesh (Jesus) after He was baptized by John and went into the wilderness for forty days & nights. (**Note***: that was Jesus's probationary period before he started His ministry and the number forty denotes probation). Read* **Matthew 3: 13-17** *(Jesus's Baptism) and* **Matthew 4:1-11** *(Jesus in the Wilderness). In order for you to read this book and check me out or try to prove me wrong you must have the proper tools to help you interpreted the prospective languages* (Hebrew, Aramaic, Chaldee and Greek) in which the King James Bible was interpreted from into English. The most important thing for me is that I stayed in constant Prayer asking the Holy Spirit to lead and guide me, and this also will help you while reading and using the tools that helped me tremendously get a full understanding. The references/tools that I used to back-up my thoughts and writings for this book are: The Companion Bible (*King James Bible version)'*, J.P. Green, Sr. *The Interlinear Bible* which is the closet you can get to the original manuscripts in *(Hebrew, Greek & English); Strong's Exhausted Concordance; Smith's Dictionary and Vines Bible Dictionary.*

When reading this book please use a King James Version (KJV) of the Bible and at least Strong's Exhausted

Concordance to get the full understanding of what I have written and the message I am sending you the reader. Not all Bibles are the same, some has been tainted, meaning words has been changed as some will say to give better flow of reading but in reality it takes away from what I believe is God's Natural Plan for Mankind before Living Eternally in His Kingdom that will be right here of Earth. Just remember every word in the Bible is not of God, but it was inspired by God to be written so you would be aware that things has be tainted for a long time and that Satan's children are always busy changing, if not, tainting the Word of God whenever and wherever he or she can. A good example is after the flood of Noah that the Kenites (Sons of Cain) where the scribes for the Tribe of Judah (King Line) in *I Chronicles 2:55?* In addition, they (Kenites) still try to mislead God's Word today. Whenever they can and however they can; most effective is through different translations of the Bible like the New International Version (NIV). Example in *Ezekiel 13:20* (KJV) God give Ezekiel the Word of warning for He knew what was too come thousands of years later (Rapture Theory). [20] *"Wherefore thus saith the Lord GOD; **Behold, I am against your pillows, wherewith ye there hunt the souls to make them*** *fly, and I will tear them from your arms, and will let the souls go, even the souls that ye hunt to make them fly." Ezekiel 13:20* (NIV) [20] *"Therefore this is what the Sovereign LORD says: I am against your magic charms with which you ensnare people like birds and I will tear them from your arms; I will set free the people that you ensnare like birds."* (Note: There is a slight difference, there is no mentioning of "hunting the Souls" and I do get the analogy of "ensnare people like birds"). Just remember it's your Soul that Satan is after and however he thinks can obtain it he's coming hard for you, but Jesus gave His Believers Power over all their enemies and Satan and his angles are enemies. Satan and his helpers always put a twist on what God has said by putting a mixture of truth and their own words that to some unlearned people it sounds good and they go with it.

Take Heed and Cut away the *Norms* and *Traditions of Men* and their *False Preaching* and *Teaching*; therefore "Circumcise Your Heart and Mind" by Guarding the Gateway to Your Ears and Eyes, because what You Hear and See will *Resonates* in Your Mind, then it goes to Your Heart. Once the Blood starts flowing from Your

Heart to Your Mind with Lies it's hard to *rejuvenate* the Mind with God's Truth!

I'm not naive; for God will put a Slumber or Stupor on *People* and it want matter how much *Truth* you give them, they just want believe.

Romans 11:8 "According as it is written, God hath given them the spirit of slumber, eyes that they should not see, and ears that they should not hear*;) unto this day." So you don't think I am scripture pulling, the* **Subject** *for Romans 8 is in the form of a question;* "Hath God cast away his people? *The* **Object** *and* **Article** *that Paul lets You and I know is that God has Seven Thousand Angles* (Seven denotes Spiritual Completeness and that can be Men & Women) *that want bow a knee to the image of Baal* **(Representative of Satan today)** *because God has a* **Remnant** *according to His* **"Election of Grace."** *(Note: When one scripture is given always read before and after that scripture).*

THE BEGINNING

A. First Earth Age (Angelica/Spiritual Beings) (Gen.1:1-2):

First Norm: For some Bible thumpers the earth is only seven or so thousand years old. Not so, the earth is millions of years old proven by Science and documented in the First Book, First Chapter & First Verse of the Bible that covers millions of years before verse two happens. *Genesis 1:1 "In the beginning God created the heaven and the earth."* This is well known to some, if not, most scholars as the *"First Earth Age;"* do not get the word *"And" that starts verse two twisted in your mind as an English reader to be a continuous of verse one, but it's the beginning of the "Second Earth Age"* If you do not agree with the statements above, hold on and keep reading because what I have to say may enlighten you and be good food for thought. In some versions of the Bible *Genesis1:1* states *"God created the Heavens and Earth",* which goes in hand why I can say *"First Earth Age"* Heavens being plural would mean *Dispensation of Time."* There's

1

only one Earth and one Heaven, but there are different ***Dispensations of Time for Both.***

That being said, the interpreter(s) explicitly place a period after verse one, and the word *"And"* that begins verse two is not a conjunction to verse one, but this *"And"* that begins verses 2-31 placing emphasis on each verse as a useful way of conveying a surprise to a new beginning. In addition, in the ***"Beginning"*** as stated in ***John 1:1-4 & 14*** *"In the beginning was the Word, and the Word was with God, and the Word was God.* ² *The same was in the beginning with God.* ³ *All things were made by him; and without him was not anything made that was* made. ⁴ In him was life; and the life was the light of men." (The **"him"** is **Jesus!**) ¹⁴ And the Word was made flesh, and dwelt among us, (and we beheld his glory, the glory as of the only begotten of the Father,) full of grace and truth." ***Question:*** Who was God speaking too in ***Genesis 1:26***? "And God (Elohim) said, Let us make man in our image, after our likeness." I have heard sermons preached and it said in Bible studies that God was speaking to Jesus and the Holy Spirit; but I propose to you God was speaking to His Angels *(You and I as Angelica Spiritual Beings). HUM!*

The first part of the *Genesis 1:26* was fully manifested when Jesus-*Yesh'ua* in the Hebrew language means *"Jehovah Saves"* was born of woman (Mary). In *Isaiah 7:13* it was foretold that a virgin shall give birth and the new born will be named Immanuel which in the English language is (Emmanuel). Emmanuel is a title--not a name and it means *"God with Us"* and Jesus was *"God with Us"* as the *"King of kings," "Lord of lords," "Almighty God," "Wonderful Counselor,"* & etc. but all of which are titles, not names.

God will *rejuvenate* the Heaven and Earth back to its original state as He created it in the *"First Earth Age"* before Satan (the Cherubim that covered the Mercy Seat) got full of pride within himself and convinced a third of God's children to follow him. Now this lead me to the *second norm* where many get it wrong believing that when God created the Earth it was as *Genesis 1:2* states, but if one ask themselves the question *"why"* instead of just reading it at face value in English then they will get the full understanding and the reason God put forth His plan for Salvation. Oh yea, when God decided to *"Destroy the First Earth Age"* He had His *"Plan of Salvation"* in motion beginning in *Genesis 1:2*; and not what most are taught that Salvation was needed because of what Adam and Eve had done in the Garden of Eden.

B. Second Earth Age (Flesh) - Creation (Adam) (Gen. 1:3-31, Gen 2, Is. 45:18):

Second norm: *Genesis 1:2* "And the earth was without form, and void; and darkness *was* upon the face of the deep. And the Spirit of God moved upon the face of the waters." The word *"was"* is **(hayah)** in the Hebrew language that means **"became"** and the words *"without form and void"* is *(tohuw va bohuw)* means vain, empty, wicked and confused wilderness. God did not create the Earth *"without form and void"* and if you believe so, then the LORD lied to Isaiah. *Isaiah 45:18 "For thus saith the LORD (YHVH) that created the heavens; God himself that formed the earth and made it; he hath established it, he created it not in vain, he formed it to be inhabited: I am the LORD; and there is none else."* Now that *you have* read that God did not create the earth void and without form there should be a question in your mind *"why **did** the earth become void and without form?"*

That being said, ***Genesis 1:2*** should be *"The earth became without form, and void; and darkness was upon the face of the deep. And the Spirit of God moved upon the face of the waters."* The earth was vain, empty, wicked and a confused wilderness because Lucifer was that (darkness) that covering cherub caused such confusion when he convinced a third of the sons of God (angels) to follow him instead of loving our Father therefore, the reason that the Spirit of God *(Holy Spirit)* moved upon the face of the waters because that was the Flood of all Floods since the ***Foundation (Katabole)*** of this Earth and the ***"Beginning"*** of God putting forth His ***"Plan of Salvation"*** into action. Those words were a mouth full and maybe mind blowing for some that Satan *(Lucifer)* convinced a third of God's Angles to follow him. Let it be known, there is a great difference in ***(Followers & Elect)****;* Satan has ***(Seven Thousand Elect Angles)***, and along with him has no chance to obtain salvation, and will be the first to be cast into the ***"Lake of Fire."*** Therefore God loving all His children decided to destroy that *"Earth Age"* instead of killing a third of His children set a *plan into action to salvage their Soul that they too may have ever lasting life with Him in Eternity.* In **Ecclesiastes 1:9***"The thing that hath been, it is that which shall be; and that which is done is that which shall be done: and there is no new thing under the sun"* **(Note:** After you read the scriptures on the following page you can form your own opinion, but remember to pray and let the Holy Spirit lead and guide your *Heart* and *Mind* towards the *Truth).* Satan rebelled and was cast out of heaven in the First Earth Age (Read Job 1:7) and now during this *"Second Earth Age"* he's in heaven held in chains behind Jesus Christ; but will be cast out again before the end of this (Flesh) Earth Age with his **Seven Thousand Lieutenants/Elect Angles.** **Isaiah 14:12:** *"How you have fallen from heaven, O morning star, son of the dawn! You have been cast down to the earth, you who once laid low the nations."* When Lucifer sinned, Jesus said, **"I saw Satan fall like lightning from heaven"** *(Luke 10:18)*, and in the book of the Revelation Satan is seen as *"a star that had fallen from the sky to the earth" (Revelation 9:1).* In addition: that one third of an **"innumerable company** *of angels" (Hebrews 12:22)* chose to rebel with him. John in *(Revelation 12: 3-9)* saw this great wonder in heaven, *"an enormous red dragon. His tail swept a third of the stars out of the sky and flung them to the earth. The great dragon was hurled down—that ancient serpent called the devil, or Satan, who leads the whole world astray. He was hurled to the earth and his angels with him."* Since Satan is referred to as a **"star"** which fell or was cast down **(Katabole)** to earth, and *(Revelation 12:4)* says a third of the **"stars"** were cast out with him, then the conclusion is that the **"stars"** in **(Revelation 12)** refer to **"angels"** who **"Followed"** him along with his **Seven Thousand Lieutenants/Elect Angles** as described in *Jude 6* who did not keep their first estate and chose not to be born of **"Woman,"** but rather came into **"Woman"** which in return gave birth to **"Giants"** who had remembrance of **"Old/First Earth Age."** I will give you a hint if you are saying to yourself: *What is the author trying to say or talking about?* This was one of the reasons behind the **"Flood"** in Noah's day, and the cause of the destruction of Sodom and Gomorrha because of unnatural sex acts between members of the same sex.

Yes, Homosexuality is not a new thing or fad; God did not approve of it then, nor does He approve of it now. ***Third norm****:* The six days mentioned of creation stated in Genesis chapter one some literally believe are a day as we live & count our days. If so, why in ***Psalms 90:4*** *"For a thousand years in thy sight are but as yesterday when it is past, and as a watch in the night?"* The cross reference to that in the New Testament is ***2 Peter 3:8*** *"But do not forget this one thing, dear friends: With the Lord a day is like a thousand years, and a thousand years are like a day?* **Food For Thought:** ***Genesis 5:27*** "And all the *days of Methuselah were nine hundred sixty and nine years: and he died!" One can say that he and every human being will not spiritually be out of* the presents of God for a full day according to God's time-line (Eternity). So put this thought to work in your mind that those six days of creation are literally Six Thousand Years, God rested for a Thousand Year and then formed ***"The Adam" (eth- ha'adham)*** whose genealogy He/Jesus Christ/The Word would be born through (become flesh by being born of a woman).

C. The Adam" and Eve "What really happen in the Garden of Eden?" (Gen. 3)

Before getting into what happen one must know why there was *"The Adam"* and Eve after God had already created man and woman (all the races) on the sixth day. The reason for *"The Adam"* and Eve being singled out from the creation of the rest of mankind is because that through the womb of Eve, umbilical cord to umbilical cord, would eventually four- thousand years later, be born the Messiah Jesus the Christ. The Bible is basically the story of one man's family and the peoples that they encounter throughout history. That is the history of *"The Adams"* family, through which Jesus Christ would come. And through the *"Sacrifice of Jesus Christ"* on the cross, all peoples from all the Nations *(eth'-nos)* in the Greek language *"New Testament,"* and **goyem** in the Hebrew language *"Old Testament"* of the earth can be grafted into the eternal family of God in the Eternity, in Heaven! It was in His (The LORD {YHVH} GOD's) image that *"The Adam"* was formed. We know this because in the New Testament Jesus is referred to as the *"The Last Adam."* The reason for this is so that there would be a direct genetic lineage from God Almighty Himself, through *"The Adam"* (whom He formed), and through Eve (whom He took from Adam's DNA); through Seth and all the way down through successive generations, umbilical cord to umbilical cord, through which would be born *Jesus Christ (who was a virgin birth from God's Holy Spirit through Mary)*. Thus Jesus Christ would be the perfect *"Lamb"* without spot or blemish and *the perfect one and once for all time sacrifice for the atonement of sins of all mankind!* Jesus was 100% man and 100% God *"Physically"* and *"Spiritually" (Genesis 1:26a "Let* **us make man in our image, after our** *likeness:"*). I propose to you that *God- Elohim* is speaking to *(You and I)* His Angles, and that we were created in the *"Image"* God wanted us to be in; the only twist is that we would be in a *"Flesh Body"* that would age, with "Mortal Souls" subject to be *"Blotted Out," "Perish"* or easily said; experience *("Second Death")*by way of the *"Lake of Fire"* unless we adhere to God's *"Salvation Plan" (Salvage of the Soul)* and become *"Immortal Souls."* This is also why Eve is referred to as the *"Mother of All Living,"* for through her would come the *"Savior of the World"*

Jesus Christ, and through Him all can live *"Eternally."* Many read that Eve was the *"Mother of All Living,"* and confuse it to mean that she was the *"First Woman."* This is not so, actually the word *"Eve"* in the Hebrew language means: *"Mother of All Living"* the Bible interpreting it for you by saying in *Genesis 3:20 "And Adam called his wife's name Eve; because she was the mother of all living."* For Eve, and all other peoples could live eternally by the fruit of her womb, *Jesus Christ*; hence it is written of Eve: *"... she shall be saved in childbearing, if they continue in faith and charity and holiness with sobriety" (1 Tim 2:13- 15).*

All the names in the Bible have meanings, and by understanding the meanings of the names in their native languages gives us deeper insight into what the meaning of certain verses are. Look in a *Smith's Bible Dictionary* will supply the meanings *(translations)* of every proper people/person and place named in the Bible, read a review of the *Smith's Bible Dictionary* as soon as you can. Now, to the very interesting topic of and coming out the gate with it one must know what *(beguile)* means and being (seduced). If you do not get this straight in your Heart and Mind then there is no way you will know who your enemies are and why God said in ***Ezekiel 3:17 "Son of man, I have made thee a watchman unto the house of Israel: therefore hear the word at my mouth, and give them warning from me."*** We too are to be Watchmen, therefore I am obligated to inform you that Satan in the role of the serpent had sex with Eve, and then Adam & Eve had sex.

Now before blowing me off and thinking I am crazy, thoroughly read **Genesis 2,** *because God never said anything about any Fruit nor Touch either* Tree. God said in ***Genesis 2:16-17 "And the LORD God commanded the man, saying, of every tree of the garden thou mayest freely eat:*** *17* ***But of the tree of the knowledge of good and evil, thou shalt not eat of it: for in the day that thou eatest thereof thou shalt surely die."*** The serpent went to Eve because God never spoke to Eve and you know how easy it is to misquote that which was spoken to you by another person. Therefore the serpent placed doubt in Eve's mind by saying in ***Genesis 3:1-5;*** *"Yea, hath God said, Ye shall not eat of every tree of the garden?"* **(Note: Then in verse 2 Eve started**

misquoting what God had said because she heard it from Adam and not God for herself:) [2] *"And the woman said unto the serpent, We may eat of the fruit of the trees of the garden:* [3] *But of the fruit of the tree which is in the midst of the garden, God hath said, Ye shall not eat of it, neither shall ye touch it, lest ye die."* **(Note: Satan knew what God had told Adam and that Eve had messed it all up, therefore the serpent (Satan) knew he could do whatever he want to do and that was to lie:)** [4] *"And the serpent said unto the woman, Ye shall not surely die:* [5] *For God doth know that in the day ye eat thereof, then your eyes shall be opened, and ye shall be as gods, knowing good and evil."*

I know you are saying ***"how do I get that the serpent had sex with Eve?"*** The word *(Touch)* is **Strong's Hebrew #5060 naga'** (naw-gah); a primitive root; properly, to touch, i.e. lay the hand upon (for any purpose; euphem, *to lie with a woman)*. The word *(beguiled)* in *Genesis 3:13* is **Strong's Hebrew #5377** nasha (naw-shaw); a primitive root; to lead astray, i.e. (mentally) to delude, or (morally) to seduce: Strong's # 1818 *exapatao (ex-ap-at-ah'o): from* 1537 and 538; to seduce wholly. ***Do not miss this for God is speaking to Satan (serpent) and the*** *word (seed) in verse 15* and in **Strong's Hebrew is #2233 Zera** and its prim root is #2232 *Zara {conceive and or make pregnant}*and **#4690 Greek orcsppa** is sperma *(sper'mah)* the male *"sperm"* by implication *{offspring}.* *Genesis 3: 14-15 "And the LORD God said unto the serpent, Because thou hast done this, thou art cursed above all cattle, and above every beast of the field; upon thy belly shalt thou go, and dust shalt thou eat all the days of thy life: [15] And I will put enmity between thee and the woman, and between thy seed and her seed; it shall bruise thy head, and thou shalt bruise his heel."* The last part of this verse is the first Prophecy given by God and only half has been fulfilled when Jesus was nailed to the cross!

Ok, you should ask yourself why did he use *Strong's # 4690* in Greek language to fit his understanding that there was sex in the Garden, I am glad you asked! Because God said in *Genesis 3: 16* Unto the woman he said, *"I will greatly multiply thy sorrow and thy conception; in sorrow thou shalt bring forth children; and thy desire shall be to thy husband, and he shall rule over thee."* Satan knew that Jesus Christ was coming through the genealogy of *"The Adam" & Eve,* so Satan tried to corrupt that seed line in which Jesus Christ would be coming through; not only him by himself, but also his **Seven Thousand Lieutenants/Elect Angles** who will never be born of woman as mention in the Book of **Jude 6** *"And the angels which kept not their first estate, but left their own habitation, he hath reserved in everlasting chains under darkness unto the judgment of the great day."*

D. Genealogy of "The Adam and Cain"- (Two Seeds): (Gen. 4 & 5):

Why in Genesis do we read that there are two genealogies, one of Adam and one of Cain? Simple answer is because Cain was not of Adam, but of Satan the (serpent) and that is why you do not read of him being in Adam's genealogy. Eve had fraternal twins Cain & Abel, and everyone knows that Cain killed Abel. That being said, it is a known fact that a woman can conceived from two different men or by the same man at a different time and have twins in one pregnancy. This is why Jesus said in **John 8:44 "Ye are of your father the devil, and the lusts of your father ye will do. He was a murderer from the beginning, and abode not in the truth, because there is no truth in him. When** *he speaketh a lie, he speaketh of his own: for he is a liar, and the father of it."*

Be Watchmen Because the names are similar!

Adam's Genealogy (Genesis 5) After Abel's death: Adam - begat	Cain's Genealogy (Genesis 4: 16-24) Cain - begat
Seth - begat	Enoch - beget
Enos - begat	Irad - begat
Cainan - begat	Mehujael - begat
Mahalaleel - begat	Lemach - begat
Jared - begat	Jabal & Jubal from his wife Adah, and Tubal-cain from his wife Zillah
Enoch - begat	
Methuselah - begat	
Lamech - begat	
Noah - begat (Shem, Ham and Japheth)	

E. The Mark of the Beast: (Gen. 4:11-15)

It belongs to the Kenites who are the Sons of Cain! *(Kenite - Hebrew word # 7014 & 7017)* **#7014 is (kajin) the name of the first child and #7017** *a Kenite or member of the tribe of Kijin - Cain; therefore those of his genealogy are the Sons of Cain.* **Genesis 4:12-16 "When thou tillest the ground, it shall not henceforth yield unto thee her strength; a fugitive and a vagabond shalt thou be in the mark. ¹³ And Cain said unto the LORD, My punishment is greater than I can bear. ¹⁴ Behold, thou hast driven me out this day from the face of the earth; and from thy face shall I be hid; and I shall be a fugitive and a vagabond in the earth; and it shall come to pass, that every one that findeth me shall slay me. ¹⁵And the LORD said unto him; therefore whoever slayeth Cain, vengeance shall be taken on him sevenfold. And the LORD set a mark upon Cain, lest any finding him should kill him. ¹⁶And Cain went out from the presence of the LORD, and dwelt in the land of Nod, on the east of Eden."**

Note: Hum, a question should come to your mind of; **"Where did the people come from who are in the land of**

Nod?" Short answer: **They are of the Sixth Day Creation of God** when *"God created both male and female and told them to replenish the earth."*

Question: If there never been anyone here before *"The Adam,"* than why would God used the words replenish the earth? Hum, don't forget about the *"First Earth Age!"*

Most people believe that *"The Mark of the Beast"* will be on their *"Forehead"* and a chip in their *"Hand"* or there about. Satan is smart enough not to place a physical *"Mark"* on anyone who is in his camp being that's what everyone believes and is looking for. *The "Mark"* in the *"Forehead"* is their *"Thinking"* and in their *"Hand"* the *"Work"* they do on Satan's behalf. Remember *Ephesians 6:12 "For we wrestle not against flesh and blood, but against principalities, against powers, against the rulers of the darkness of this world, against spiritual wickedness in high places."* Pray for the Holy Spirit to Lead and Guide you to *"All Truths"* and for the gift of *"Discernment"* because there will be people who claim to be a Christian will be deceived and Jesus state in *Matthew 7:23 "And then will I profess unto them, I never knew you: depart from me, ye that work iniquity."*

F. Why did God cause a flood in Noah's Day? (Gen 6)

Genesis 6:1-7 "And it came to pass, when men began to multiply on the face of the earth, and daughters were born unto them. [2] That the sons of God saw the daughters of men that they were fair; and they took them wives of all which they chose. [3] And the LORD said, "My spirit shall not always strive with man, for that he also is flesh: yet his days shall be an hundred and twenty years [4] There were giants in the earth in those days; and also after that, when the sons of God came in unto the daughters of men, and they bare children to them, the same became mighty men which were of old, men of renown. [5] And GOD saw that the wickedness of man was great in the earth, and that every imagination of the thoughts of his heart was only evil continually. [6] And it repented the LORD that he had made man on the earth, and it grieved him at his heart. [7] And the LORD said, I will destroy man whom I have created from the face of the earth; both man, and beast, and the creeping thing, and the fowls of the air; for it repenteth me that I have made them." (Prophecy)

This is one of the reason why God caused the flood to come in Noah's day: **Jude: 5-6** *"I will therefore put you in remembrance, though ye once knew this, how that the Lord, having saved the people out of the land of Egypt, afterward destroyed them that believed not. 6 And the angels (Fallen Angles) which kept not their first estate, but left their own habitation, he hath reserved in everlasting chains under darkness unto the judgment of the great day." (***Note:*** These **"Fallen Angels"** are the **"sons of God"** spoken of in *Genesis 6:2* that works for Satan and their purpose was to destroy the seed line that Jesus Christ would be birth through**)**.

Please don't forget about Sodom and Gomorrah and all the homosexual acts that is an Abomination in God's Eyes; He didn't approve of it then, nor does He approve of it now. Go ahead and play the word game *"Civil Rights"* and we'll see what God really thinks! In addition; some believe that all the races of people came after the *"Flood"* and through Noah's three sons; if so, we all would be of the Adamic race because Noah's family was. No, God began over with the Hebrew race being that there were eight *{new beginning}* of them. These Fallen Angles *(Seven Thousand)* who decided not to be born of woman, but rather took woman for themselves and had sex with them and the outcome were children [giants who had some recall of old *{First Earth Age}* tried to corrupt the seed line of *"The Adam."*

Therefore God commanded Noah take two of every flesh (are not people flesh?) aboard the arch to continue on with God's "Plan of Salvation," and through Noah and his family because they were of pure Pedigree (ancestry line) by keeping the seed line of "The Adam," the Hebrews and later known as Israel pure for Jesus Christ to be born through. That being said, then why do we read about Kenites (sons of *Cain) in* *I Chronicles 2:55 "And the families of the scribes who dwelt at Jabez were the Tirathites, the Shimeathites, and the Suchathites. These were the Kenites who came from Hammath, the father of the house of Rechab." I'll let you draw your own conclusion, but remember God created all the races "at the same time" in Genesis 1:26-28 and He did not say that one would have dominion over the other. That brings a question*

to my mind, "so why do some people think that they are the "Supreme Race?" That is not so according to "God's Plan for Mankind," and still in 2016 it behooves me that "Racism" is as strong as it ever has been, but has been "White Washed" to some extent. Ok, that's for another book to come!

The Parable of the Fig Tree: (Mat. 24:32, Gen. 3:7, Jer. 24:2, Mic. 4:4, Rev. 6:13)

The Parable of the Fig Tree is a parable that Jesus said in *Matthew 24:32 "Now learn a parable of the fig tree; When his branch is yet tender, and putteth forth leaves, ye know that summer is nigh."* The *"Parable of the Fig Tree"* began in the *"Garden of Eden;"* being that *"The Adam"* and *"Eve"* where in a fig grove because when they knew they were naked they covered their private parts with fig leaves. *Genesis 3:7 "And the eyes of them both were opened, and they knew that they were naked; and they sewed fig leaves together, and made themselves aprons."*

Jeremiah 24:2 "One basket had very good figs, even like the figs that are first ripe: and the other basket had very naughty figs, which could not be eaten, they were so bad." Jeremiah the prophet was shown two baskets of figs. One basket had very good figs, even like the figs that are first ripe: and the other basket had very naughty [or wicked, evil] figs, which could not be eaten, they were so bad" (verse 2). In this parable, the bad figs were those people of Judah who rebelled against God and refused to go into captivity in Babylon, which the LORD had ordained for that time; while the good figs complied with the direction of the LORD and were saved. These good and evil figs also hark back to the *"Tree of the Knowledge of Good and Evil"* in the Garden of Eden, showing that the link of the fig with that tree is correct. I believe that in symbol *(while the actual tree was an olive)* it was this tree on which Jesus Christ was crucified on, as it was the Jewish leaders in his day who claimed to be Jews, but was of the bad figs *(Kenites),* who incited the populous and persuaded the Roman governor, Pilate, to order his execution. But God, in His unfathomable wisdom, ordained that the death of His only begotten Son who would atone for the sins of the world, not just of Judah and of Israel, but of "All mankind" since the day that *"The Adam"* fell from grace that is from the realm of spirit, into the realm of carnality and death. Thus, by

Jesus's sacrifice, atonement was made for the fall and the ***"Tree of the Knowledge of Good and Evil"*** which had occasioned that fell was overcome, once and for all.

The ***"Smyrna Fig"*** is one of the Good Fig Trees in the Middle Eastern area and you can parallel it to one of the two good churches in which Jesus spoke highly of in: ***Rev. 2: 7- 9 "He that hath an ear, let him hear what the Spirit saith unto the churches; To him that overcometh will I give to eat of the tree of life, which is in the midst of the paradise of God. [8] And unto the angel of the church in Smyrna write; These things saith the First and the Last, Which was dead, and is alive; [9] I know thy works, and tribulation, and poverty, (but thou art rich) and I know the blasphemy of them which say they are Jews, and are not, but are the synagogue of Satan. [10] Fear none of those things which thou shalt suffer: behold, the devil shall cast some of you into prison, that ye may be tried; and ye shall have tribulation ten days: be thou faithful unto death, and I will give thee a crown of life.[11] He that hath an ear, let him hear what the Spirit saith unto the churches; He that overcometh shall not be hurt of the second death."***

Note: Read *Revelation 2 & 3* where Jesus gives examples of Good & Bad Churches, total of 7 *(Spiritual Completeness)* whereby *2 are Good and 5 are Bad.*

Jeremiah 8 13 "I will surely consume them, saith the LORD: there shall be no grapes on the vine, nor figs on the fig tree, and the leaf shall fade; and the things that I have given them shall pass away from them." Jesus is a witness unto what God had spoken being that He is *"The Word"* that became flesh; therefore in *Matthew 21:19 "And when he saw a fig tree in the way, he came to it, and found nothing thereon, but leaves only, and said unto it, Let no fruit grow on thee henceforward forever. And presently the fig tree withered away."* The *"fig tree"* is the emblem of the Jewish nation, which seemed to be thriving with an abundance of leaves but spiritually it was producing no fruit.

In *Mark 11: 12-14* the wording is a little different from *Matthew 21:19*, when Jesus found no fruit on the tree in *Mark 11:14& 20:* He said unto it, *14"No man eat fruit of thee hereafter forever."* And the next morning his disciples *20"saw the fig tree dried up from the roots".* This phrase, *"dried up from the roots"* I believe refers back to the *"Tree*

of the Knowledge of Good and Evil" and in other words, the **"Tree"** that occasioned the fall is to be completely eradicated, and it will at the **"End",** but until then, Jesus has given us just as He did His Disciples **"Power over Satan & his Angles."**

In **Matthew 21:21-22 "Jesus answered and said unto them, Verily I say unto you, If ye have faith, and doubt not, ye shall not only do this which is done to the fig tree, but also if ye shall say unto this mountain, Be thou removed, and be thou cast into the sea; it shall be done. ²² And all things, whatsoever ye shall ask in prayer, believing, ye shall receive."**

Gifts of the Holy Spirit: (I Cor. 12:7-14 & I Cor.14:5)

I Cor. 12: 7-14 *"But the manifestation of the Spirit is given to every man to profit withal. ⁸For to one is given by the Spirit the word of wisdom; to another the word of knowledge by the same Spirit; ⁹To another faith by the same Spirit; to another the gifts of healing by the same Spirit; To another the working of miracles; ¹⁰to another prophecy; to another discerning of spirits; to another* **divers kinds of tongues***; to another the interpretation of* *tongues: But all these worketh that one and the selfsame Spirit, dividing to every man severally as he will. [12] For as the body is one, and hath many member, and all the members of that one body, being many, are one body: so also **is** Christ: [13] For by one Spirit are we all baptized into one body, whether **we be** Jews or Gentiles, whether **we be** bond or free; and have been all made to drink into one Spirit. [14] For the body is not one member, but many."* The nine gifts mention in I Corinthians are not the complete list of the *"Gifts of the Holy Spirit,"* whereby others can be found in *(Romans 12:6-8 & Ephesians 4:11-12).* Paul is telling the Corinthians that the grace of God was given unto them in Jesus Christ so that they would not be lacking in any spiritual gifts. Since every Christian has been given the Holy Spirit, he/she has the potential to demonstrate the particular gift which has been given to him/her. The intent was to exhort the Corinthians to seek God's grace and then it would be revealed further through the manifestation of the gift(s) that God will give them.

Just as the Corinthians, Christ Jesus by way of the Holy Spirit has given "all" that believe in and on Him these same gifts. For those who have adventure to read further in Romans and Ephesians, I am very aware that the gifts mentioned in Ephesians are the Fivefold Ministry which is a gift given by God without repentance. Although God does the given, but in order for the manifestation of the gift(s) to take place *"The Fruit of the Spirit"* must be in front of it because there is a war between your flesh and spirit, therefore read *Galatians 5:16-26* for there are *"nine fruits"* mentioned just as there were nine spiritual gifts mentioned in *I Corinthians*. The number spiritual significance of *"Nine"* denotes *Finality of Judgement; it is 3 x 3 the product of Divine completeness.* **Note:** The number nine, or its factors or multiples is seen in all cases when "judgement" is the subject. Remember what Paul said: **1** *Corinthians 14:5* "I would that ye all spake with tongues, but rather that ye prophesied: for greater is he that prophesieth than he that speaketh with tongues, *except he interpret, that the church may receive edifying."*

Note: There are some that think if a person does not speak in what they call tongues they are not saved and or have no power. My question is *"Who put God in a box?" He gives the Gift(s) as He sees fits and does not repent on it!*

Is it the "Cloven Tongues" or "Gibberish" You are Speaking?

I'm asking this question because we are approaching the End Times/Second Advent or I should say we are in the Last *(Fig Tree)* Generation in which our Lord Jesus Christ will be coming back, and if what is being taught and practice as *"Speaking in Tongues"* is not in accordance to the Word of God, then it needs to stop. I have asked God to show me in His Word about "Speaking in Tongues," so what I want to do is share what has been revealed to me by God through my studies, and not *"Tradition of Men."* The bottom Line Question: *Are You "Speaking" or is the Holy Spirit speaking through you?* What I have read in the Word *(Acts 2; 10; & 19)* that it was the Holy Spirit that spoke through them and it went out in *"every language of the listeners," even down to their dialect*. It was not the people themselves doing the "Speaking in Tongues" when they felt it needed to be done, or try to show others that they are holy and say that they are speaking to God!

The issue of *"Speaking in Tongues"* it's nothing for you or I to fall out over and we can still be Brother & Sister in

Christ, but let's get this correct because it's a sin to misguide God's children. According to the Strong's Exhausted Concordance of the King James Bible Greek #1100 - Glossa (gloce-sah') *"Tongues"* is a language (especially one naturally unacquired), and Greek #2084 -states other tongued, i.e., a foreign language. These two definitions are used as tongues in the New Testament of the Bible, and the listeners heard in their *"own language"* is Greek #2398 - meaning *"his own"* and in laymen's term *"dialect."* On the *"Day of Pentecost"* there were no unknown tongue spoken, but it was unknown to the mouths that were being used by the Holy Spirit to speak. Also man added the word *"unknown"* and all the words that are in '"Italics" in the King James Bible were added by man so that it would carry on the conversation thinking it would be better understood in English.

Gibberish or I can even say babel is a rapid nonsensical chatter, or a confused noise typically that's made by a number of voices. Remember *1 Corinthians 14:33a "For God is not the author of Confusion"* and if an unbeliever or one of little knowledge was to walk in a church and a person is *"so call speaking in tongues"* (to God) or trying to impress others that he/she is filled with the Holy Spirit is misleading themselves and the assembly. ***Will the Holy Spirit speak through people?*** The answer is YES, but not to show off.

The Holy Spirit is the Power that Jesus left for us to continue His work in this earth age. ***I Corinthians 14:18 "I thank my God, I speak with tongues more than ye all:"*** This scripture like many is taken out of context, because the Apostle Paul is saying that he speaks in more foreign languages then they all, for he could speak Roman, Greek, Arabic, Chaldee plus his natural language Hebrew tongue at any given time without an interpreter so he wished that we all could. ***The Holy Spirit first speaks through man collectively.*** Read ***Acts 2:1-6,*** when the ***"Day of Pentecost"*** had fully come was the first time the Holy Spirit spoke through men collectively. The ***"other tongues"*** (#1100 - naturally unacquired language) that was spoken on that day by them that were in the house as the Holy Spirit gave them utterance was done even in the dialect of those who were listening. Where: All the languages that were spoken are in verses *(Acts 2: 9-11),* so there is nothing unknown about these tongues/languages that were spoken. The ***"Pentecost Tongue"*** or ***"Cloven Tongue"*** is best described as if you were speaking at the

United Nations and everyone could understand you in their own language without the need for an interpreter, that would be the evidence of the Holy Spirit, and no man can fake that.

What was the gift of tongues in the Bible?

It was and still is the supernatural *(Holy Spirit)* that controls the tongue to speak in a language that had never been learned by the person doing the speaking. This happens in accordance too the guidance of the Holy Spirit to deliver a message from God therefore it's an unknown tongue to the speaker and he/she more than likely do not know what was said **(Acts 2:5-8,11)**. The word *"tongue"* means *"language"* and The *"gift of tongues"* was and is not the ability to speak in a string of *"gibberish" or "babbling;"* There is nothing supernatural about that and it profits nobody and can easily be faked or simply learned. How many times do we see the *"gift of tongues"* exercised in God's Word? There are only *"three instances in the entire Word of God where the gift of tongues"* is actually exercised, and they are in *(Acts 2, 10, & 19)*. With the exception of the book of *(I Corinthians)*, the *"gift of tongues"* is never referred to in any other Epistles of Paul.

What was the purpose of the gift of tongues?

God sheds great light on the purpose of the *"gift of tongues"* in *I Corinthians 14:22.* It clearly states, *"Wherefore tongues are for a sign, not to them that believe, but to them that believe not:"* One thing is clear. The *"gift of tongues"* was a sign to and for unbelievers. In context (vs. 22), it is obvious that Paul had unbelieving Israelites in mind. When we cross reference it with *I Corinthians 1:22*, we find that the *"Jews require a Sign!"* The nation of Israel was born through the use of miraculous signs *(Exodus 4:30-31).* Because of their stubbornness and unbelief, God has always dealt with Israel through the use of miraculous signs. *(Psalm 74:9)* In the Old Testament, *"strange tongues were a sign to Israel of impending judgment." (Isaiah 28:11-12; Jeremiah 5:15; Deuteronomy 28: 15-68)*

The Bible is clear *"tongues"* are for a sign, the Jews required a sign and to put it simply, the *"Gift of Tongues"* was a sign to Israel in the book of Acts and this may explain why we never see *"tongues"* spoken unless there were Jews present. The gift was never given as a means of personal edification *(heavenly prayer language)* as some call it and I would like to know where that is stated in the Bible. It was a gift used to get *God's truth out and to be a sign to Israel.* Tongues are never spoken - or even mentioned - outside of the Acts time period, because Israel's program was set aside in *(Acts 28: 26-28), 1 Corinthians was written during the book of Acts.*

How does the story of Peter and Cornelius fit in with all of this teaching about tongues?

When the apostles were filled with the Spirit in *Acts 2 (First Time & Witness),* the Holy Spirit spake through them immediately in *"cloven tongues" meaning it went out in all the languages of the people who were present* (Acts 2:4-8). This was a miraculous sign to Israel that authenticated the apostles' message and the fact that they were filled with God's Spirit. *(Second Time & Witness)*When Cornelius and his entire house of Gentiles believed Peter's message, God immediately gave those Gentiles the Holy Spirit. But how would Peter know this? God gave these Gentiles the "same gift" that He gave to Peter and the twelve on the *"Day* *of Pentecost"* the *"gift of tongues"* Cornelius being a Roman leader of soldiers, he would have known Latin, and maybe some Greek in which Peter and the other Jews would recognized it, so it may have been Aramaic or Hebrew that they spoke, who knows for it is not said, but one thing for sure it was a language that was not of their natural *"tongue."* This was the outward, visible, miraculous sign to Peter and the other Jews with Peter that these Gentiles had, in fact, truly received God's Spirit as those on the *"Day of Pentecost"* and there was no denying it *(Acts 10:44-46).* When Peter had to give an account to his Jewish brethren at Jerusalem, it was the sign *"gift of tongues"* that kept Peter out of hot water *(Acts 11:15-18).* There are those who would like to take this story and try to make it the standard for every person that gets saved and Filled/Baptized with the Holy Spirit; but this is quite ludicrous because God is the one who chooses which *"Gift"* is given to a person who believes In and On His Son Jesus Christ by Faith. Therefore, who in these days are the *"Tester(s) & Witness(es)"* of a *"True Pure Language"* being spoken that was not learned? Witnesses

This was a unique, one-of-a-kind event. These Gentiles *"spoke in tongues"* to outwardly demonstrate to Peter and all the believing/unbelieving Jews that God had, in fact, given His Holy Spirit to these Gentiles by faith alone. This was a groundbreaking event that would require a miraculous sign to convince the Jews of its validity. This event would be crucial for the future of the church and for Paul's ministry to the Gentiles. At the Jerusalem Council, it was this event that Peter would refer back to in demonstrating that the Gentiles do not have to keep the Jewish law to be saved, and that Gentiles should be included in the church by grace through faith alone *(Acts 15:7-11). (Third Time Witness) of the "Cloven Tongues" (Acts 19:1-7)* was when John the Baptist (twelve) disciples where *"Baptized in the name of the Lord Jesus and when Paul laid his hands upon them, the Holy Spirit came on them: and they spake with tongues, and prophesied."*

Fact: The Holy Spirit will speak that *"Cloven Tongue"* again, it was done as a sign to the unbelievers in those days, as well for the *"gainsayers"* that will be here when the *Elect (Men and Women)* are delivered up before the *"Synagogue of Satan"* of them who wish to persecute them in that *"Hour of Temptation"* read *(Mark 13: 9 -11, Luke 21:12 -15, 1 Corinthians 14: 22, and Revelation 17:12).*

In addition: I also will add that the Holy Spirit will speak through mankind when it is necessary for a message to be delivered to one who does not understand or speak your natural language. ***This can happen in "two ways;"*** **one** is that the *(hearer/receiver)* hears the words being spoken in their own language as the person who is doing the speaking is speaking in their own language and *two,* just as it happen on the *"Day of Pentecost"* the person that is speaking the unknown language that was not taught to him/her is by the power of the Holy Spirit. The main thing I'm trying to get across is that it's the *Holy Spirit* that does the speaking not the person himself/herself. There are Christians who believe that when the Pastor says *"pray in the spirit,"* he or she is saying *"speak with tongues"* and they *"automatically start speaking what they believe to be speaking in tongues"* and the humorous thing about it is that only God can understand it I suppose. That is a perception that is wrong, for what is the *"Gift of Tongue"* for? People please read the scriptures!

Yes, there is a guarantee time that the Holy Spirit will speak "Cloven Tongues" again as He did in Acts 2, Jesus tells us when it will happen in *Matthew 10: 16-20: "Behold, I send you forth as sheep in the midst of wolves: be ye therefore wise as serpents, and harmless as doves. [17] But beware of men: for they will deliver you up to the councils, and they will scourge you in their synagogues; [18] And ye shall be brought before governors and kings for my sake, for a testimony against them and the Gentiles. [19] But when they deliver you up, take no thought how or what ye shall speak: for it shall be given you in that same hour what ye shall speak. [20] For it is not ye that speak, but the Spirit of your Father which speaketh in you."*

Note: *If you are one of God's Elect and you refuse to let the Holy Spirt to speak through you when delivered up before Satan and his Elect Angles, this sin is the only sin that is "Unforgivable."*

Again, Jesus states in *Matthew12:31-32; "Wherefore I say unto you, All manner of sin and blasphemy shall*

be forgiven unto men: but the blasphemy against the Holy Ghost shall not be forgiven unto men. [32] **And whosoever speaketh a word against the Son of man, it shall be forgiven him: but whosoever speaketh against the Holy Ghost, it shall not be forgiven him, neither in this world, neither in the world to come."**

I know you may question my reasoning because Jesus said *"blasphemy"* and I say "does not allow" is the same. The word blasphemeo is from a compound word *blásphemos* (New Testament (NT): 989) and *blásphemos* means, "to BE abusive and revile another's good name." The word *blásphemos* is a compound of two root words, *"blapto,"* (NT: 984) and *"pheme"* (NT: 5345). Blapto is a primary verb meaning, to hinder, i.e. to injure. Pheme (pronounced "fame") is from a root word "phemi" (NT: 5346) and means, "a saying, i.e. rumor," and phemi originates from phos (NT: 5457) and "phaino" (NT: 5316), which means, "to reveal or make one's thoughts known thru speech." Combining all of the literal meanings of all the words that make up the Greek blasphemeo, a precise definition of the word translated as "blasphemy" in the (NT).

Think what you must, don't let us fallout over that, so put it on the shelf, come back and pray about it and keep opening the Word of God up!

Jesus End Time Warnings: (7 Seals, Trumps & Vails)! (Matthew 24:1-16, 19- 25; Mark 13 & Luke 21: 6-28)

Jesus gives the reader *(You & I)* and His Disciples what's going to happen when things are about to be wrapped up and made as it was in *"The Beginning,"* because He will be returning as the *"King of kings"* and *"Lord of lords."* Now I will let the Word *(Jesus)* speak, so the Holy Spirit can *"Circumcise Your Heart and Mind."*

Matthew 24:1-16, 19-25; "And Jesus went out, and departed from the temple: and his disciples came to him for to shew him the buildings of the temple. [2] And Jesus said unto them, See ye not all these things? Verily I say unto you, there shall not be left here one stone upon another that shall not be thrown down. [3] And as he sat upon the Mount of Olives, the disciples came unto him privately, saying, Tell us, when shall these things be? and what shall be the sign of thy coming, and of the end of the world? [4] And Jesus answered and said unto them, Take heed that no man deceive you. [5] For many shall come in my name, saying, I am Christ; and shall deceive many. [6] And ye shall hear of wars and rumors of wars: see that ye be not troubled: for all these things must come to pass, but the end is not yet. [7] For nation shall rise against nation, and kingdom against kingdom: and there shall be famines, and pestilences, and earthquakes, in diver's places. [8] All these are the beginning of sorrows. [9] Then shall they deliver you up to be afflicted, and shall kill you: and ye shall be hated of all nations for my name's sake. [10] And then shall many be offended, and shall betray one another, and shall hate one another. [11] And many false prophets shall rise, and shall deceive many. [12] And because iniquity shall abound, the love of many shall wax cold. [13] But he that shall endure unto the end, the same shall be saved. [14] And this gospel of the kingdom shall be preached in all the world for a witness unto all nations; and then shall the end come. [15] When ye therefore shall see the abomination of desolation, spoken of by Daniel the prophet, stand in the holy place, whoso readeth, let him understand:"

(Note: Read *Daniel 9: 23-27; Daniel 11: 36-38 & Daniel 12:11)* [16] "Then let them which be in Judaea flee into the mountains: [19] And woe unto them that are with child, and to them that give suck in those days!" *(Note:* The phase **"them that are with child"** is talking about those who worship *Satan (Anti-Christ)* thinking he is *Jesus Christ* and are pregnant with his word; a deeper meaning is like a man has been gone from his wife for years and comes back and she is with child she has been unfaithful to him. Remember Jesus Christ is coming back and there's going to be a wedding and His Bride has to be a Virgin Spiritually.) [20] *"But pray ye that your flight be not in the winter, neither on the sabbath day:* (**Note**: Don't be harvest out of season, the harvest is from May to September and the Sabbath was set aside by God for man to rest) [21] "For then shall be great tribulation, such as was not since the beginning of the world to this time, no, nor ever shall be. [22] And except those days should be shortened, there should no flesh be saved: but for the elect's sake those days shall be shortened." *(Note:* The days were shorten from 7 years to 5 months, read *Revelation 9:5 & 10)* [23] *"Then if any man shall say unto you, Lo, here is*

Christ, or there; believe it not. [24] For there shall arise false Christs, and false prophets, and shall shew great signs and wonders; insomuch that, if it were possible, they shall deceive the very elect. [25] Behold, I have told you before." It is very important that you read and cease not praying about **Mark 13** and **Luke 21** and you can see for yourself that Jesus had told us about how it will be before He comes for His **"Bride,"** for the **"Wedding"** and the end of this *"Earth Age."* In addition; He also told John in the ***Book of Revelation chapters 5 – 18*** about these things.

Two Tribulations: (Satan's & God's)

This is the last chapter of the book and it may be the most important one, because if you do not know the characteristics of your main enemy *(Satan)* then you are fighting a losing battle. Many people believe that *"The Anti-Christ"* will be born and I have even heard the question *"is he here now?"* Satan will not be born of woman and he definitely will not allow anyone to take his position as *"The Instead of Christ is The Anti-Christ"* because he wants to take as many people/souls as he can into the Lake of Fire with him. Note: When reading the entire chapter of *Ezekiel 28* stay focus on whom God is speaking to *Ezekiel* about, because in reality there was a *"Prince of Tyrus & King of Tyrus."* In addition, the word Tyrus comes from Tyre and when it's transliterated it means *"rock"* but not our *"Rock."* Now some *History on Tyre*: It was an ancient *Phoenician city,* about 23 miles, in a direct line, north of *Acre*, and 20 miles south of Sidon. *Sidon was the oldest Phoenician city*, but *Tyre* had a longer and more illustrious history. Tyre consisted of two distinct parts, a rocky fortress on the mainland, called *"Old Tyre,"* and the city built on a small rocky island about half-a-mile distant from the shore. *It was a place of great strength*, and *the commerce of the whole world was gathered into the warehouses of Tyre.* I give you this information so when reading you can understand *why Satan chooses certain places toward accomplishing his mission.*

1. The Anti-Christ & Two Witness (Eze. 28, Mat. 24, Mark 13 and Rev 9) & (Rev 11)

I began in *Ezekiel 28:12-19* because this describes Satan's characteristics before God demoted and past sentence on him. Just keep in mind that Jesus said in

Luke 10:19 "Behold, I give unto you power to tread on serpents and scorpions, and over all the power of the enemy: and nothing shall by any means hurt you." [12] *"Son of man, take up a lamentation upon the king of Tyrus, and say unto him, Thus saith the Lord GOD; Thou sealest up the sum, full of wisdom, and perfect in beauty."* [13] *"Thou hast been in Eden the garden of God; every precious stone was thy covering, the sardius, topaz, and the diamond, the beryl, the onyx, and the jasper, the sapphire, the emerald, and the carbuncle, and gold: the workmanship of thy tabrets and of thy pipes was prepared in thee in the day that thou wast created.* [14] *Thou art the anointed cherub that covereth; and I have set thee so: thou wast upon the holy mountain of God; thou hast walked up and down in the midst of the stones of fire.* [15] *Thou wast perfect in thy ways from the day that thou wast created, till iniquity was found in thee.* [16] *By the multitude of thy merchandise they have filled the midst of thee with violence, and thou hast sinned: therefore I will cast thee as profane out of the mountain of God: and I will destroy thee, O covering cherub, from the midst of the stones of fire.* [17] *Thine heart was lifted up because of thy beauty, thou hast corrupted thy wisdom by reason of thy brightness: I will cast thee to the ground, I will lay thee before kings, that they may behold thee. [18] Thou hast defiled thy sanctuaries by the multitude of thine iniquities, by the iniquity of thy traffick; therefore will I bring forth a fire from the midst of thee, it shall devour thee, and I will bring thee to ashes upon the earth in the sight of all them that behold thee. [19] All they that know thee among the people shall be astonished at thee: thou shalt be a terror, and never shalt thou be any more."*

You may still think that God is actually talking about a man that was king of Tyrus, but take notice that I italicized some words that gives you a clear understanding who God was telling *Ezekiel* to take up a lamentation against. If not convinced that it was Satan because it reads king of Tyrus, then in **verse 13** *"hast been in Eden the garden of God"* gives you the reader its first hint that it was Satan who was in **Genesis** as the *"tree of Knowledge of good and evil"* (Satan's plays the role as the serpent). **Verse 14** gives a more definitive description of Satan and not a man king, *"art the anointed cherub that covereth."* Before God demoted Satan and sentence was passed on him in **verse 18** *"therefore will I bring forth a fire from the midst of* **thee"** meaning that he has a first class ticket to the *"Lake of Fire"* and his mission is to take as many people/souls as he can with him. Now we go to Satan's characteristics/description of him in this presence time, and how his sentence will be passed on him after the Millennium. **Ezekiel 28: 1-10**. *"The word of the LORD came again unto me, saying,* [2] *Son of man, say unto the prince of Tyrus, Thus saith the Lord GOD; Because thine heart is lifted up, and thou hast said, I am a God, I sit in the seat of God, in the midst of the seas; yet thou art man, and not God, though thou set thine heart as the heart of God:* [3] *Behold, thou art wiser than Daniel; there is no secret that they can hide from thee:* [4] *With thy wisdom and with thine understanding thou hast gotten thee riches, and hast gotten gold and silver into thy treasures: they shall defile thy brightness.* [5] **By thy great wisdom and by thy traffick hast thou increased thy riches, and thine heart is lifted up because of thy riches:** [6] **Therefore thus saith the Lord GOD; Because thou hast set thine heart as the heart of God;"** [7] **"Behold, therefore I will bring strangers upon thee the terrible of the nations:**

and they shall draw their swords against the beauty of thy wisdom, and *⁸ They shall bring thee down to the pit, and thou shalt die the deaths of them that are slain in the midst of the seas. ⁹ Wilt thou yet say before him that slayeth thee, I am God? but thou shalt be a man, and no God, in the hand of him that slayeth thee. ¹⁰ Thou shalt die the deaths of the uncircumcised by the hand of strangers: for I have spoken it, saith the Lord GOD.*

Another example from the Old Testament is from *Isaiah 14: 12-15: "How art thou fallen from heaven, O Lucifer, son of the morning! how art thou cut down to the ground, which did weaken the nations! ¹³For thou hast said in your heart, I will ascend into heaven, I will exalt my throne above the stars of God: I will sit also upon the mount of the congregation, in the sides of the north: ¹⁴I will ascend above the heights of the clouds; I will be like the most High.¹⁵ Yet thou shalt be brought down to hell, to the sides of the pit."*

(*Note:* So the **Prince of Tyre** was the anointed cherub that fell from grace in heaven!!! Now he has the form of a man, with his own little territory to himself, and now that Satan has been described from the beginning to the end, let's see what Jesus said how he will come back and play the role of Christ and be "The Anti-Christ.")

There are *"Two Witnesses"* of this, one being in *Matthew 24:15; 21-24 and Mark 13: 5-8; 19-27.* I start with *Matthew 24:15* "**When ye therefore shall see the abomination of desolation, spoken of by Daniel the prophet, stand in the holy place, whoso readeth, let him understand:**" To understand we go to *Daniel 11:21-24:* "And in his estate shall stand up a vile person, to whom they shall not give the honour of the kingdom: but he shall come in *peaceably,* and *obtain the kingdom by flatteries.* ²² *And with the arms of a flood shall they be overflown from before him, and shall be broken; yea, also the prince of the covenant.* ²³ *And after the league* made *with him he shall work deceitfully: for he shall come up, and shall become strong with a small people.* ²⁴ *He shall* **enter peaceably** *even upon the fattest places of the province; and he shall do* that *which his fathers have not done, nor his fathers' fathers; he* shall **scatter among them the prey, and spoil, and riches:** *yea, and* *he shall forecast his devices against the strong holds, even for a time.*

Now the actual ***"Tribulation of Satan"*** (**Note:** that within this Jesus shorten the original time of *Satan's* tribulation to five months*)* can be found in and tells the reader why in) ***Matthew 24: 21-24; "For then shall be great tribulation, such as was not since the beginning of the world to this time, no, nor ever shall be.*** *²²* ***And except those days should be shortened, there should no flesh be saved: "but for the elect's sake those days shall be shortened.*** *²³* ***Then if any man shall say unto you, Lo, here is Christ, or there; believe it not.*** *²⁴* ***For there shall arise false Christs, and false prophets, and shall shew great signs and wonders; insomuch that, if it were possible, they shall deceive the very elect."***

In **Revelation 9:5** *Jesus gives use the period of time for Satan's entire tribulation;* *⁵* ***"And to them it was given that they should not kill them, but that they should be tormented five months: and their torment was as the torment of a scorpion, when he striketh a man."*** In *Mark 13 we find the* ***"Second Witness"*** *of what Jesus said to His disciples pertaining to how the end time shall* *come into existence and "The Anti-Christ" playing Jesus Christ.*

Mark 13 19-25: "For in those days shall be affliction, such as was not from the beginning of the creation which God created unto this time, neither shall be. [20] And except that the Lord had shortened those days, no flesh should be saved: but for the elect's sake, whom he hath chosen, he hath shortened the days.[21] And then if any man shall say to you, Lo, here is Christ; or, lo, he is there; believe him not:" [22] For false Christs and false prophets shall rise, and shall shew signs and wonders, to seduce, if it were possible, even the elect. [23] But take ye heed: behold, I have foretold you all things. [24] But in those days, after that tribulation, the sun shall be darkened, and the moon shall not give her light, [25] And the stars of heaven shall fall, and the powers that are in heaven shall be shaken (**Note:** *Satan and his Seven Thousand Angles/Elect are the "stars" and power that fall to earth.*) In *Revelation 12: 7-12* is the *"Third Witness"* to *"The Anti-Christ"* coming before Jesus. Jesus gave John the vision of what had happened that caused the *"Katabole"- meaning the falling down and the "Beginning of this Second Earth & Heaven Age/*

Dispensation of Time." As stated in ***Ecclesiastes 1:9*** *"The thing that hath been, it is that which shall be; and that which is done is that which shall be done: and there is no new thing under the sun."*

In addition, in ***Revelation 12:9*** all the names of Satan are given to take heed of the role each play and be the ***"Watchman"*** that God called you to be. ***Revelation 12: 7-12*** *"And there was war in heaven: Michael and his angels fought against the dragon; and the dragon fought and his angels, ⁸ And prevailed not; neither was their place found any more in heaven. ⁹ And the great dragon was cast out, that old serpent, called the Devil, and Satan, which deceiveth the whole world: he was cast out into the earth, and his angels were cast out with him. ¹⁰ And I heard a loud voice saying in heaven, Now is come salvation, and strength, and the kingdom of our God, and the power of his Christ: for the accuser of our brethren is cast down, which accused them before our God day and night.¹¹ And they overcame him by the blood of the Lamb, and by the word of their testimony; and they loved not their lives unto the death.¹² Therefore rejoice, ye heavens, and ye that dwell in them. Woe to the inhabiters of the earth and of the sea! for the devil* *is come down unto you, having great wrath, because he knoweth that he hath but a short time."* **(Note:** That *"short time"* has been *"shorten"* to *"Five Months"* as stated in *Rev. 9:5).*

Two Witnesses:

The **"Two Witnesses"** will be on earth before Satan arrival to forewarn God's people of what's about to happen; in addition, some scholars believe as I do that the **"Two Witnesses"** are *(Moses - The Law Giver)* and *(Elijah - The Prophet)* who was on *"Mount of Transfiguration"* in their **"Transfigured Body"** with **Jesus** who was in *"His Transfigured Body"* in *Matthew 17.* This will be explain and brought out in paragraphs to come; the only other person that was *"taken"* and descended into *"Heaven"* without *"Death"* was **Enoch.** *Revelation 11:3-4 "And I will grant authority to my two witnesses, and they will prophesy for "twelve hundred and sixty days," clothed in sackcloth. ⁴ These are the "two olive trees" and the "two lampstands" that stand before the Lord of the earth."*

(**Note:** The connection between this vision of the two preachers and the previous passage *(verses 1-2)* should be clear). They are among *"God's Unique Witnesses"* who will proclaim His message of judgment during the final stages of the Gentile trampling on Jerusalem and will *"Preach the Gospel"* so that the *"Jewish Remnant"* can believe and enjoy God's protection.

Witnesses: is the plural form of *"martus,"* from which the English word martyr derives, since so many witnesses of Jesus Christ in the early church paid with their lives. Since it is always used in the New Testament to refer to persons, the two witnesses must be actual people, not movements, as some commentators have held. There are *"Two Witnesses"* because the Bible requires the testimony of two people to confirm a fact or verify the truth *(Deut. 17:6; 19:15; Matt. 18:16; John 8:17; 2 Cor. 13:1; 1 Tim. 5:19; Heb. 10:28).* The *"Two Witnesses"* responsibility is to prophesy. Prophecy in the New Testament does not necessarily refer to predicting the future. Its primary meaning is *"to speak forth, to proclaim, to preach, and or to teach."* The *"Two Witnesses"* will proclaim to the world that the disasters occurring during the *"last half* *of the Tribulation"* are the judgments of God. They will warn that God's final outpouring of judgment and eternal hell will follow. At the same time, they will preach the gospel, calling people to repentance and faith in the Lord Jesus Christ. The period of their ministry is twelve hundred and sixty days, *"the last three and one-half years of the Tribulation;* (**Note:** *Remember this time span also was shorten by Jesus because He shorten Satan's* "Anti-Christ" *time here or no flesh would be save as Jesus described earlier)* when the *"Anti-Christ"* forces oppression on the city of Jerusalem *(Rev. 12:2),* and many Jews are sheltered in the wilderness *(Rev 12:6).* The fact that they are actual preachers and not symbols of institutions or movements is indicated by the description of their clothing.

Rev.11: 3-6 "And I will give power to my two witnesses, and they will prophesy one thousand two hundred and sixty days, clothed in sackcloth" ⁴ *These are the two olive trees and the two lampstands standing before the God of the earth.* ⁵ *And if anyone wants to harm them, fire proceeds from their mouth and devours their enemies. And if anyone wants to harm them, he must be killed in this manner.* ⁶ *These have power to*

shut heaven, so that no rain falls in the days of their prophecy; and they have power over waters to turn them to blood, and to strike the earth with all plagues, as often as they desire."

The question *"Who are the Two Witnesses"* has intrigued Bible scholars over the years, and numerous possibilities have been suggested. John identifies them merely as the *"two olive trees"* and the *"two lampstands"* that stand before the Lord of the earth. That enigmatic description is drawn from *Zechariah 4:1-14. Zechariah's* prophecy looks forward to the restoration of Israel in the Millennium *(Zech. 3:8-10).* The *"olive trees"* and *"lampstands"* symbolize the *"Light of Revival,"* since olive oil was commonly used in lamps. The connecting of the lamps to the trees is intended to depict a constant, spontaneous, automatic supply of oil flowing from the *olive trees* into the *lamps*. That symbolizes the *"Truth"* that God will not bring salvation blessing from human power, but by the power of the Holy Spirit *(Zech. 4:6).* Like *Joshua* and *Zerubbabel,* the *"Two Witnesses"* will lead a *"Spiritual Revival"* of Israel culminating in the building of a temple. Their preaching will be instrumental in Israel's national conversion *(Rev.11:13; Rom. 11:4-5, 26),* and the temple associated with that conversion will be the *"Millennial Temple."*

While it is impossible to be dogmatic about the specific identity of these two preachers, there are a number of reasons that suggest that they may be Moses and Elijah.

FIRST, the miracles they will perform *(destroying their enemies with fire, withholding rain, turning water into blood, and striking the earth with plagues)* are similar to the judgments inflicted in the Old Testament by God through *Moses* **and** *Elijah* for the purpose of stimulating repentance. *Elijah* called down *"Fire"* from heaven *(2 Kings 1:10, 12)* and pronounced a *"three-and-one-half-year"* drought on the land *(1 Kings 17:1; James 5:17)* the same length as the drought brought by the *"two witnesses"* (Rev. 11:6). *Moses* turned the *"Waters"* of the Nile into *"Blood"* *(Ex. 7:17-21)* and announced the other plagues on Egypt recorded in *Exodus chapters 7&12.*

SECOND, both the Old Testament and Jewish tradition expected *Moses* and *Elijah* to return in the future. *Malachi 4:5* predicted the return of *Elijah,* and the Jews believed that God's promise to rise up a prophet like *Moses (Deut. 18:15, 18)* necessitated his return *(John 1:21; 6:14; 7:40)*. *Jesus'* statement in *Matthew 11:14 "if you are willing to accept it, John (the Baptist) himself is Elijah who was to come"* does not necessarily preclude *Elijah's* future return. Since the Jews did not accept Jesus, John did not fulfill that prophecy, but came *"in the spirit and power of Elijah, to turn the hearts of the fathers back to the children, and the disobedient to the attitude of the righteous, so as to make ready a people prepared for the Lord" (Luke 1:17)*.

THIRD, both *Moses* and *Elijah (Representing the Law and the Prophets)* appeared with *Jesus Christ* on *"Mount Transfiguration,"* the preview of the *Second Coming (Matt. 17:3?)*.

FORTH, both left the earth in unusual ways; *Elijah* never died, but was transported into heaven in a **fiery chariot (2 Kings 2:11-12),** and God supernaturally buried *Moses'* body in a secret location *(Deut. 34:5-6; Jude 9)*. **HUM!** The statement of *Hebrews 9:27* *"it is appointed for men to die once and after this comes judgment"* does not rule out Moses' return, since there are other rare exceptions to that general statement such as Lazarus

(John 11:14, 38-44). Since the text does not specifically identify these *two preachers,* the view defended above, like all other views regarding their identity, must remain speculation.

2. Rapture Theory (I Thes 4:13-17 & II Thes. 2:1-12)

The etymology of the word *"Rapture"* is derived from Middle French *rapture,* via the Medieval Latin *raptura ("seizure, kidnapping"),* which derives from the Latin *raptus ("a carrying off").* The Koine Greek of *1 Thessalonians 4:17* uses the verb form ἁρπαγησόμεθα *(harpagisometha),* which means *"we shall be caught up"* or *"taken away",* with the connotation that this is a sudden event. The dictionary form of this Greek verb is *harpazō (ἁρπάζω).* This use is also seen in such texts as *Acts 8:39, II Corinthians 12: 2-4* and *Revelation 12:5.* The Latin Vulgate translates the Greek ἁρπαγησόμεθα as *rapiemur,* from the verb *rapio* meaning *"to catch up"* or *"take away".*

(**NOTE:** The King James Bible was not interpreted from Latin writings, but from Hebrew, Aramaic, Chaldee, and Greek Languages. The Rapture doctrine did not exist before John Darby along with some other so call preachers invented it in 1830 AD; and before it "popped into their head's no one had ever heard of a secret rapture doctrine**).**

The word **Rapture** is not in the Bible, but it is a popular term used to describe one perceived view of the return of Jesus based on the writings of the **I Thessalonians 4:17** "Then we which are alive and remain shall be caught up together with them in the clouds, to meet the Lord in the air: and so shall we ever be with the Lord."

Before going further I must break down some words into the original language so you can get clear understanding of what the Apostle Paul was really saying. In addition, you must read before verse 17 to get the Subject of this part of the letter. One must understand that Apostle Paul spoke **slang** Greek and I will give you an example from one of his writing's especially pertaining to how he used the word **"cloud."** *First* **word too set straight in your mind is "Air"** used in verse 17: from Strong's Exhausted Concordance Air: {1 Th. 4:17} Greek #109 aer (ah-ayr'); from aemi (to breathe unconsciously, i.e. respire; by anal.

to blow); Compare #5594 Greek word psucho: meaning to blow, to make cool. In a nut shell this **"Air"** that Apostle Paul is writing about is **NOT** the Atmosphere/Sky; but the same as when God breathe or blew into mankind's nostrils that gave him/her life **(Breath of Life).** Hum, if you cannot handle that, then put it on the shelf and now let me give you that example of *Apostle Paul's slang for cloud. In Hebrew 12:1* *"Wherefore seeing we also are compassed about with so great a cloud of witnesses,"* this is a "large gathering of people. When Jesus returns every living thing that has breath will become spiritual beings, and remember *"every knee shall bawl"* at His coming, and those who believe In and on Jesus will gather together in a large crowd. This happens because they had withstood Satan's tactics and their Faith in God that He would be Faithful by His Word for Salvation of them that Believed. Now let's go to the subject and get the entire text in which Apostle Paul was writing to the Thessalonians about.

The subject starts in **I** *Thessalonians 4: 13-16* *"But I would not have you to be ignorant, brethren, concerning them which are asleep, that ye sorrow not, even as others which have no hope.*[14] *For if we believe* *that Jesus died and rose again, even so them* also *which sleep in Jesus will God bring with him.* [15] *For this we say unto you by the word of Lord, that we which are alive and remain unto the coming of the Lord shall not prevent them which are asleep.*[16] *For the Lord Himself shall descend from heaven with a shout, with the voice of the archangel, and with the trump of God: and the dead in Christ shall rise first:"* (**Note:** this was a bad interpretation of what was written because **"the dead in Christ"** has already risen. Remember verse 14, therefore verse 16d is a contradiction of the Word, God forbid**).** That being said I believe it to be the ideal spiritual condition of believers in regard to sin, if not, it has contradicted verse14. Pray!

II Thessalonians 2: 1-12; *"Now we beseech you, brethren, by the coming of our Lord Jesus Christ, and by our gathering together unto him,* [2] *That ye be not soon shaken in mind, or be troubled, neither by spirit, nor by word, nor by letter as from us, as that the day of Christ is at hand.*[3] *Let no man deceive you by any means: for that day shall not come, except there come a falling away first, and that man of sin be revealed, the son of perdition;* (**Note:** No other than Satan himself, because he is the only one named to perish which means perdition. Remember what God said in ***Ezekiel 28:18c "therefore will I bring forth a fire from the midst of thee, it shall devour thee, and I will bring thee to ashes upon the earth in the sight of all them that behold thee.")*** *⁴ Who opposeth and exalteth himself above all that is called God, or that is worshiped; so that he as God sitteth in the temple of God, shewing himself that he is God. ⁵ Remember ye not, that, when I was yet with you, I told you these things? ⁶ And now ye know what withholdeth that he might be revealed in his time. ⁷ For the mystery of iniquity doth already work: only he who now letteth will let, until he be taken out of the way. ⁸ And then shall that Wicked be revealed, whom the Lord shall consume with the spirit of his mouth, and shall destroy with the* **brightness of his coming:** *⁹ Even him, whose coming is after the working of Satan with all power and signs and lying wonders, ¹⁰And with all deceivableness of unrighteousness in them that perish; because they received not the love of the truth, that they might be saved. ¹¹ And for this cause God shall send them strong delusion, that they should believe a lie: (Note: God is speaking about Christians who want to hang onto Traditions of Men) ¹² That they all might be damned who* *believed not the truth, but had pleasure in righteousness."*

In addition, to sum it up God, gave Ezekiel His Word that has come to pass in our generation today especially when using different translations to teach the people to believe a lie.

Ezekiel 13: 1-7, 17-23; *"And the word of the LORD came unto me, saying,* ² *Son of man, prophesy* **say thou unto them that prophesy out of their own hearts, Hear ye the word of the LORD;** ³ **Thus saith the Lord GOD; Woe unto the foolish prophets, that follow their own spirit, and have seen nothing!** ⁴ **O Israel, thy prophets are like the foxes in the deserts.** ⁵ **Ye have not gone up into the gaps, neither made up the hedge for the house of Israel to stand in the battle in the day of the LORD.** ⁶ **They have seen vanity and lying divination, saying, The LORD saith: and the LORD hath not sent them: and they have made others to hope that they would confirm the word.** ⁷ **Have ye not seen a vain vision, and have ye not spoken a lying divination, whereas ye say, The LORD saith it; albeit I have not spoken?"**

(Note: *Remember I told you in a paragraph above that John Darby along with some other so call preachers* *invented it and started preaching it in 1830 AD; these preachers had* stolen this theory from a Scottish girl named ***Margaret MacDonald who had a "so call vision"*** from God about the ***"Pretribulation"*** and they called it ***"Rapture"*** when they was finish with it. It was easier for them to teach and preach it for everyone to accept this Lie because it was from man; in those days no one would believe a woman because it was and still is taught in some churches that women are not to teach or preach God's Word).

Here is what God had said about this lie:

Ezekiel 13: 17-23; "Likewise, thou son of man, set thy face against the daughters of thy people, which prophesy out of their own heart; and prophesy thou against them, [18] And say, Thus saith the Lord GOD; Woe to the women that sew pillows to all armholes, and make kerchiefs upon the head of every stature to hunt souls! Will ye hunt the souls of my people, and will ye save the souls alive that come unto you? [19] And will ye pollute me among my people for handfuls of barley and for pieces of bread, to slay the souls that should not die, and to save the souls alive that should not live, by your lying to my people that hear your lies? ²⁰ Wherefore thus saith the Lord GOD; Behold, I am against your pillows, wherewith ye there hunt the souls to make them fly, and I will tear them from your arms, and will let the souls go, even the souls that ye hunt to make them fly. ²¹ Your kerchiefs also will I tear, and deliver my people out of your hand, and they shall be no more in your hand to be hunted; and ye shall know that I am the LORD. ²² "Because with lies ye have made the heart of the righteous sad, whom I have not made sad; and strengthened the hands of the wicked, that he should not return from his wicked way, by promising him life: ²³ Therefore ye shall see no more vanity, nor divine divinations: for I will deliver my people out of your hand: and ye shall know that I am the LORD"

Don't get it twisted, most educated preachers will preach **Ezekiel 13:17-23** from the NIV translation and when you get to verse 20 it says something about **"Bird."** Now I wonder who came up with that, could it have been the **Kenites (sons of Cain)** that I spoke about who were scribes for the **Tribe of Judah (King Line)** in *I Chronicles 2:55?* Hum!

3. The Lord's Day - Millennium (Ezekiel 40-48, and Rev. 20)

This is what all Christians are looking forward too, the return of Jesus Christ to set this world in *"Order."* The Lord's Day is known as *"The Second Advent"* of Jesus Christ, and this will not happen until "The Two Witnesses" are dead for three days lying in the arena where they were killed. Then the Seventh Trump will sound and Jesus will arrive with His Army and every living thing that has breath will become spiritual beings and for humans *"every knee shall bawl"* at His coming, and those who believe In and On Jesus will gather together in a large crowd. (**Note:** *There's that "Cloud")*

To fully get a clear understanding of *"The Lord's Day"* one must read *Ezekiel 40-48* over and over until it sinks into your spirit and let God give you *"Revelation"* knowledge of what's really being said. Once you receive the *"Revelation"* that God's Holy Spirit shows you, then there is more in *Ezekiel 40-48* than in *Revelation 20.* The *"Second Advent"* of Jesus will last for a thousand years, and every person who had died beforehand and was on the *"Left"* side of the *"Gulf"* in *"Paradise"* and those who are alive before they are/were changed into their *"Spiritual Body"* that was not gathered together in the crowd when Jesus return will be taught the *"Truth"* and nothing but the *"Truth and Discipline"* of God's Word. Now let's see what the Word of God says what will happen during and after *"The Lord's Day"* in *Revelation 20*.

Revelation 20: 1-15; *"And I saw an angel come down from heaven, having the key of the bottomless pit and a great chain in his hand. [2] And he laid hold on the dragon, that old serpent, which is the Devil, and Satan, and bound him a thousand years, [3] And cast him into the bottomless pit, and shut him up, and set a seal upon him, that he should deceive the nations no more, till the thousand years should be fulfilled: and after that he must be loosed a little season. [4] And I saw thrones, and they sat upon them, and judgment was given unto them: and I saw the souls of them that were beheaded for the witness of Jesus, and for the word of God, and which had not worshipped the beast, neither his image, neither had received his mark upon their foreheads, or in their hands; and they lived and reigned with Christ a thousand years.[5] But the rest of the dead lived not again until the thousand years were finished. This is the first resurrection. [6]Blessed and holy is he that hath part in the first resurrection: on such the second death hath no power, but they shall be priests of God and of Christ, and shall reign with him a thousand years.[7] And when the thousand years are expired, Satan shall be loosed out of his prison, [8] And shall go out to deceive the nations which are in the four quarters of the earth, Gog and Magog, to gather them together to battle: the number of whom is as the sand of the sea. [9] And they went up on the breadth of the earth, and compassed the camp of the saints about, and the beloved city: and fire came down from God out of heaven, and devoured them. [10] And the devil that deceived them was cast into the lake of fire and brimstone, where the beast and the false prophet are, and shall be tormented day and night for ever and ever.[11] And I saw a great white throne, and him that sat on it, from whose face the earth and the heaven fled away; and there was found no place for them.[12] And I saw the dead, small and great, stand before God; and the books were opened: and another book was opened, which is the book of life: and the dead were judged out of those things which were written in the books, according to their works. ¹³ And the sea gave up the dead which were in it; and death and hell delivered up the dead which were in them: and they were judged every man according to their works.¹⁴ And death and hell were cast into the lake of fire. This is the second death.¹⁵ And whosoever was not found written in the book of life was cast into the lake of fire."* **(Note:** In *(Rev. 20: 1 - 3d)* you notice that Satan and all his names and positions are in the bottomless pit for a thousand years; that being said and everyone is in their *"spiritual body"* with full recall and no evilness to bother them are taught the *"Truth and Discipline"* on the ways to please God and have life everlasting in Eternity right here on Earth. Then in verse *(Rev. 20:3f) "Satan"* will be loose for a season and believe it or not, there still will be those who will follow Satan straight into the *"Lake of Fire"* and be *"Blotted Out"* know more and will experience *"The Second Death"* as described in *(verse 14).* Those who do not follow Satan will also be judge according to their *"Works"* as described in *(verse 12)* and will inherit life in Eternity with the Full Godhead right here on Earth. Remember the Prayer that Jesus taught us to pray and some people call it the Lord's Prayer (Wrong) has come into **"Full Circle"** because Thy Kingdom has Come here on Earth in Jerusalem as it was in the **"Beginning!"**

"The Chose is Yours, What You Going to Do?"

Summary

This book was written to inform everyone that there has been and still are *"Untruths"* being preached and taught in churches today and if your spirit is not in touch with God's Holy Spirit then you will be *"Deceived"* *as Jesus had already told you not too be* and may end up following the *"Anti-Christ"* straight into *"The Lake of Fire."* One example of a big deception are the *"Pictures of Jesus Christ"* being portrayed as a *"White"* person; NO person alive has seen Jesus Christ and they will not print Jesus Christ as a *"Black"* person or as described in *Revelation 1:14-15; "His head and [his] hairs [were] white like wool, as white as snow; and his eyes [were] as a flame of fire; [15]And his feet like unto fine brass, as if they burned in a furnace;"* now is that description of someone who is **"White"** or **"Black?"** NO, but sure enough not as portrayed as it is written in the Bible!

People out of ignorance do not read and believe what is presented to them through pictures, illustrations or twisting the Word to fit their ideology. That being said,

Satan will come however you believe Jesus or whoever you believe to be your Savior according to your faith too look like. I tried to create the flow of *"Truths"* that will be of great help to prepare you for that Great Day that is to come and it gets closer Day by Day. Jesus cannot come back until *"All"* things that's written has come to pass in the *"Order"* in which God's Holy Spirit inspired men to write what is In and On God's Heart. I believe if a person does not know what happen in the *"Beginning"* of this *"Earth Age;"* then he or she will not understand what is too come at the *"Second Advent"* of Jesus Christ and the *"End"* of this *"Earth Age."* Therefore I give you a very short synopsis of the two pieces of "Bread" that holds the middle in place as a reminder!

Genesis 1:2 *"And the earth was without form, and void; and darkness was upon the face of the deep."* (**Note:** Using the Strong's Concordance to break down the Hebrew transcript it should read *("And the earth became {tohuw va bohuw} vain, empty, wicked and confused wilderness and darkness was upon the face of the deep).* The earth became void; God did not create it that way! Something or someone caused utter confusion to come upon the earth. **Proof, *Isaiah 45:18* *"For thus saith the Lord that created the heavens; God Himself that formed the earth and made it; He hath established it, He created it not in vain, he formed it to be inhabited: I am the Lord; and there is none else!"***

Lucifer, that covering Cherub *(Hierarchy of Archangels)* was that *"darkness"* and He caused God to *"Destroy"* that *"First World (Earth) Age."* [Stop, hold on and ask yourself how come we now have *"Two Norths" {Magnetic North and True North}, Jet Streams, Four Seasons of Weather and etc.*]. (**Note:** *Archangels and Cherubims are the Elite of God's Spiritual Beings and will not ever be born of woman as the rest of His Angles/Souls have and has to be*)**!** Lucifer (the great dragon, that old serpent, called the Devil, and Satan, which deceiveth the whole world): was one of God's most Beautiful and Wise Sons made in the full pattern as described in *(Ezekiel 28),* but He became vain *(proud and conceited)* and wanted to be as God and sit on the Mercy Seat that was and is reserved for Jesus Christ. He pulled one third of the sons of God with him and caused them to follow him, instead of loving our Father. In **(Rev. 12:4)** Our Father was so hurt by this, that He had a choice to either destroy the third of the Souls/ Angles who followed Satan or destroy/ put to end that *"First World (Earth) Age"/ (Dispensation of Time)* that was *"Spiritual."* **(Note***:* We now live in the *"Second World (Earth) Age"/ (Dispensation of Time)* in the *"Flesh Body"* and according to *(Gen. 6:5-7)* [5] *"And GOD saw that the wickedness of man was great in the earth, and that every imagination of the thoughts of his heart was only evil continually.* [6] *And it repented the LORD that he had made man on the earth, and it grieved him at his heart.* [7] *And the LORD said, I will destroy man whom I have created from the face of the earth; both man, and beast, and the creeping thing, and the fowls of the air; for it repenteth me that I have made them."* Yes, God has a Heart! With that said there is nothing new under the Sun according to *(Eccl. 1:9)* "The thing that hath been, it *is that* which shall be; and that which is done *is* that which shall be done: and there is no new *thing* under the sun." **(Note:** The thing that hath been will be in the *"Third (World) Age"/ (Dispensation of Time)*, *"Spiritual"* again after the *"Great White*

Throne Judgment" and there will not be any Evilness found, and God will Rejuvenate the Earth and setup His Kingdom right here on Earth. **Hallelujah!**

God so Loved His children that instead of destroying their Souls, He put His *"Plan of Salvation"* into action and have every Soul be birth innocent through the womb of woman *(That's the First Baptism of the Soul)* in this *"Second (Flesh) World (Earth) Age"/(Dispensation of Time).* God passed sentence of *"The Second Death"* in the *"First World (Earth) Age"/ (Dispensation of Time)* on Lucifer *(Son of Perdition, Serpent, Satan, Dragon, Devil, (Prince & King Tyrus), "The Anti-Christ"). Abaddon in the Hebrew tongue* and *Apollyon in the Greek tongue (Rev. 9: 11),* along with his *Seven Thousand Lieutenants (Angels)* after they refused to be born of woman and left their first estate *Jude 6 "And the angels which kept not their first estate, but left their own habitation, he hath reserved in everlasting chains under darkness unto the judgment of the great day."* They did so to seduce woman because that was the new thigh God had made and it was beautiful while at the same time lustful to them and they had to have it *(God created woman from man using his "Feminine*

Part of DNA," not Rib); and yes, they just as Satan impregnated women *and that's how the Giants came about and one of the reasons for the flood in Gen. 6:9 - 9:17.*

If you did not know it, Satan is supernatural and when he comes as Jesus Christ, he will make things happen that only one would believe that God can do. In addition, he will have the biggest *"Revival"* the world has ever seen or heard of and that which is the *"Norms"* for many teachings will be manifested so they will believe he is Jesus Christ. The *"Word"* said that the *"Whole World"* will follow after him and this is why Jesus had to shorten the time to five months *(Rev. 9:5)* or there would be no flesh saved because of the many different roles Satan will play and may even fool the Elect. Let's see what Jesus said, and remember He's not talking about the Soul and Spiritual Body! *Matthew 24: 20-24; "But pray ye that your flight be not in the winter, neither on the sabbath day: ²¹For then shall be great tribulation, such as was not since the beginning of the world to this time, no, nor ever shall be. ²² And except those days should be shorten, there should no flesh be saved: but for the elect's sake those days shall be shortened. ²³ Then if any man shall say unto you, Lo, here [is] Christ, or there; believe [it] not. ²⁴For there shall arise false Christs, and false prophets, and shall shew great signs and wonders; insomuch that, if [it were] possible, they shall deceive the very elect."*

I have given you a lot of meat between the slices of bread of this sandwich I want you to eat, just remember there is no *"Rapture -Flying"* away because God has equipped His Saints with the Word, and all the Armour they will need to defeat their enemies. I did not see any *"Jet-Pack"* in that list of *"Armour"* in *(Eph.6: 10-18).* But thank God in the name of Jesus Christ *(Yeshua)* meaning God's Savior; we who believe Jesus gave us **"Power"** over *"All"* our *"Enemies,"* and as long as we *"Endure Until Our End"* we shall be saved and inherit Eternal life. Therefore stay in constant Prayer, guard Your Ears & Eyes Gate and when necessary go into Your Closet or Quit Place and let God's *Holy Spirit "Circumcise Your Heart and Mind!"*

All *"SOULS"* belongs to GOD and You have Free Will too Choose to Love GOD or Follow Satan?

IT'S YOUR SALVATION, JESUS GAVE US THE POWER, LEARN HOW TO USE IT. SPIRITUALLY CIRCUMCISE YOUR HEART AND MIND!

**It is Finish When the Holy Spirit Flows
from Your Heart to Your Mind!**

Appendix

Where to Find the 7 Seals, Trumps & Vails

#	Seals	Trumps	Vails
1	Rev. 6:1	Rev. 8: 7	Rev. 16: 2
2	Rev. 6:3	Rev. 8: 8	Rev. 16: 3
3	Rev. 6: 5	Rev. 8: 10	Rev. 16: 4
4	Rev. 6:7	Rev. 8:12	Rev. 16:8
5	Rev. 6:9	Rev. 9:1	Rev. 16:10
6*	Rev. 6:12	Rev. 9:13	Rev. 16:12
7**	Rev. 8:1	Rev. 11:15	Rev. 16:17

NOTE: The asterisks indicate <u>666 </u>(number of man) the time frame and events that will happen when Satan will appear in ''body form" as a supernatural being, claiming to be Jesus Christ, but instead is the Anti-Christ. This is when the Seals, Trumps, and Vails all line up chronology. Also important to mention, the Seals are not in chronology order, but rather they are given in such order for teaching purposes.

We are now in the Fifth Seal (Teaching to Seal the Hearts and Minds with Truth)!

The Spiritual Significance of Numbers

Reference is from "The Companion Bible" (KJV) Appendix 10

One - Denotes Unity, and Commencement. The first occurrences of words or utterances denote their essential significance, in interpretation. First Day, Light.

Two - Denotes Difference. If two different persons agree in testimony it is conclusive. Otherwise two implies opposition, enmity, and division, as was the work of the Second day.

Three - Denotes Completeness, as three lines complete perfection and completeness.

Four - Denotes Creative Works (3+1), and always has reference to the material creation, as pertaining to the earth, and things "under the sun," and things terrestrial.

Five - Denotes Divine Grace. It is (4+1). It's God adding His gifts and blessing to the works of His hands. It's the leading factor in the Tabernacle measurements.

Six - Denotes the Human Number. Man was; created on the sixth day; and was the first occurrence of the n umber makes it (and all multiples of it) the hall-mark of all connected with man. He works six days. The hours of His day are a multiple of six.

Seven - Denotes Spiritual Perfection. I t is the number or hall-mark of the Holy Spirit work. He is the Author of God's Word, and seven is stamped on it as the water-mark is seen in the manufacture of paper. He is the Author and Giver of life; and seven is the number, which regulates every period of Incubation and Gestation, in insects, birds, animals, and man.

Eight -Denotes Resurrection, Regeneration; a new beginning or commencement. The eighth is a new first. It is the number that has to do with the Lord, Who rose on the eighth or new "first-day. "This therefore, the (Dominical Number - Of or associated with Christ as the Lord; and relating to Sunday ac; the Lord's Day.)

Nine -Denotes Finality of Judgement. It is (3X3), the product of Divine Completeness. The number nine, or its factors or multiples are seen in all cases when judgement is the subject.

Ten - Denotes Ordinal Perfection. Another new first; after the ninth digit, when numeration commences anew.

Eleven - Denotes Disorder, Disorganization, because it is one short of the number twelve (see below).

Twelve - Denotes Government Perfection. It is the number or factor of all numbers connected with government: whether by Tribes or Apostles, or in measurements of time, or in things which have to do with government in the heavens and earth.

Thirteen - Denotes Rebellion, Apostasy, Defection, Disintegration, and Revolution. The first occurrence fixes this (Gen. 14 4); and the second confirms it (Gen. 17:25).

Seventeen -Denotes a combination of Spiritual and Order (10 + 7). It is the seventh prime number (13 is the sixth prime number).

NOTE: Other numbers follow the Law which governs the smaller numbers, as being their Factors, Sums, Products or Multiples: e.g.

24 = (12 x 2) A higher form of 12.

25 = 5^2 Grace Intensified

27 = 3^3 Divinity Intensified

28 = 7 x 4 Spiritual Perfection in connection with the Earth

30 = 3 x 10 Divine Perfection applied to Order

40 = 10 x 4 Divine Order applied to earthly things. Hence, the number of Probation.

<u>**The Four Perfect Numbers**</u>: **<u>3, 7, 10</u>** and <u>12</u>, have for their product the remark number **<u>2,520</u>**. It is the Least Common: Multiple of the ten digits governing all numeration; and can, therefore, be divided by each of the nine digits, without a remainder. It is the number of Chronological Perfection (**<u>7 x 360</u>**).

Books of the Bible And Their Meaning & Time Period

THE OLD TESTSMENT		
The Law (Torah)/*The Five Books of the Pentateuch*		
Title	Meaning	Time Period
Genesis	"Bereshith" – In the Beginning	4,000 B.C.
Exodus	"veelleh shemoth - Redemption	1,446 B.C.
Leviticus	"vayyikra – Worship	1,445 B.C.
Numbers	"Bemidbar" – In the Wilderness	1,444 B.C.
Deuteronomy	"Haddebarim" – The Word	1, 406 B.C.
The History		
Joshua	"Yahsus" (Jesus) – Yahveh (GOD) the Savior	1,406 B.C.
Judges	"Shophetim" – Rulers	1,380 B.C.
Ruth	A Story of Loyalty	1,200 B.C.
I Samuel	"Shemuel" – Asked of God	1,105 B.C.
II Samuel		1,010 B.C.
I Kings	The Kingdom United	970 B.C.

Title	Meaning	Time Period
II Kings	The Kingdom Divided	848 B.C.
Title	Meaning	Time Period
I Chronicles	Dibrei hayyamim – Words of the Days	1,000 B.C.
II Chronicles		970 B.C.
Ezra	Born in Confusion	538 B.C.
Nehemiah	Comforter of Yahveh (GOD)	445 B.C.
THE OLD TESTSMENT		
Esther	"Estthur" – The Hidden Star	479 B.C.
Job	"Iyyob" – Persecuted	2,000 B.C.
Psalms	"Tehillim" – Songs, to Rejoice	1,000 B.C.
Proverbs	"Mishlai" – To Rule	970 B.C.
Ecclesiastes	"Koheleth" – The Preacher	940 B.C.
Song of Soloman	"Shir Hashshirim" – Songs of Songs	970 B.C.
Isaiah	Salvation of Yahveh (GOD)	740 B.C.
Jeremiah	Launches Forth	626 B.C.
Lamentations	One God Sends Forth	586 B.C.

| Ezekiel | "Yehezkel" – El is Strong | 1,446 B.C. |
| Daniel | GOD my Judge | 605 B.C. |

| THE OLD TESTSMENT | | |
| *The Minor Prophets* | | |
Title	Meaning	Time Period
Hosea	"Hoshea" – Salvation	750 B.C.
Joel	Yahveh (GOD) is GOD	835 B.C.
Amos	Burden	760 B.C.
Obadiah	Servant of Yahveh (GOD)	855 B.C.
Jonah	Warmth of a Dove	785 B.C.
Micah	Who is like Yahveh (GOD)?	740 B.C.
Nahum	The Compassionate, or Consoler	620 B.C.
Habakkuk	To Embrace	605 B.C.
Zephaniah	Hidden of Yahveh (GOD)	635 B.C.
Haggai	Feast of Festival	520 B.C.
Zechariah	Remembered of Yahveh (GOD)	520 B.C.
Malahhi	My Messenger	440 B.C.

THE NEW TESTSMENT		
The Four Gospels		
Matthew	Jesus, The True King	6 B.C.
Mark	Jesus, The Servant of All	26 A.D.
Luke	Jesus, The Man of Compassion	6 B.C.
John	Jesus, The Son of God	26 A.D.
Acts	The Acts of the Apostles	30 A.D.
The Epistles		
Title	**Meaning**	**Time Period**
Romans	God's Plan to Save Mankind	57 A.D.
I Corinthians	The Problems of the Church in Corinth	55 A.D.
II Corinthians	Paul Answers His Accusers	56 A.D.
Galatians	Christianity as a Reality, not "Traditions"	49 A.D.
Epheshians	We are One in Christ	60 A.D.
Philipians	Serve Others with Joy	61 A.D.

Colossians	Jesus is Above All Things	60 A.D.
I Thessalonians	Encouragement for New Christians	51 A.D.
II Thessalonians	The Return of Christ	52 A.D.
I Timothy	Advice to a Young Preacher	64 A.D.
II Timothy	Encouragement to a Soldier of Christ	66 A.D.
Titus	Instructions for Doing Good	64 A.D.
Philemon	A Slave becomes a Christian	60 A.D.
Hebrews	A Better Life through Christ	66 A.D.
James	How to Live as a Christian	49 A.D

THE NEW TESTSMENT		
The Four Gospels		
Title	Meaning	Time Period
I Peter	Written to God's Elect	62 A.D.
II Peter	Correcting False Teachings	67 A.D.
I John	The Lover of God	90 A.D.

II John	Beware of the False Teachers	90 A.D.
III John	Love to those who Walk in the Truth	90 A.D.
Jude	Warnings of Evil Men and False Teachers	65 A.D.
The Apocalypse		
Revelations	"apokalupsis" – to Reveal, Prophesy	95 A.D.

I give you "Books of the Bible" with its Meaning and Time Period, so you will have an understanding what a particular "Book" means; therefore, when you are studying or wondering what to read when you are in a situation and need a Word from God you know where to go.

Let it be known that there are Sixty-Six "Books" and there are Sixty-Six "Chapters" in the Book of Isaiah, Hum!